A SHAKESPEARE LOVER'S DIARY

SHAKESPEARE LOVER _____

DIARY KEPT BETWEEN _____ AND _____

A SHAKESPEARE
LOVER'S DIARY

FIREFLY BOOKS

A Shakespeare Lover's Diary
ISBN 1-55209-406-5

A FIREFLY BOOK
Published by Firefly Books Ltd., 3680 Victoria Park Avenue, Willowdale, Ontario, Canada M2H 3K1

Published in the U.S. by Firefly Books (U.S.) Inc.
P.O. Box 1338, Ellicott Station, Buffalo, New York 14205

Conceived and edited by Shelagh Wallace
Design and original illustrations by Scott McKowen

Acknowledgements
We wish to thank those publishers who have given their permission to reproduce excerpts from works still in copyright. If anyone has been unintentionally omitted, we offer our apologies and ask that you notify the publisher so you may be included in future editions.

Quotations by Laurence Olivier from *On Acting*, reproduced by permission of the publisher, Weidenfeld and Nicolson, UK.

Quotations by Northrop Frye reprinted with permission from *Northrop Frye on Shakespeare* ©Northrop Frye, published by Fitzhenry & Whiteside, Markham, Ontario.

Quotation by George Bernard Shaw reprinted by permission of The Society of Authors, on behalf of the Bernard Shaw Estate.

Quotation by Harley Granville Barker from *Prefaces to Shakespeare*. Copyright ©1947, renewed 1975, reprinted by permission of Princeton University Press.

Quotation by Bertolt Brecht reproduced by permission of Routledge, Inc. Copyright ©1973 Stefan S. Brecht. Translation copyright ©1993 Stefan S. Brecht. Introduction and editorial notes from this edition copyright ©1993 Methuen London. Copyright ©1993, ©1996. From BERTOLT BRECHT JOURNALS: 1934-1955 ed. John Willett and Ralph Manheim.

Quotation by John Hirsch reprinted by permission of The Stratford Festival and the estate of John Hirsch.

Quotations from *The Friendly Shakespeare* by Norrie Epstein (New York: Penguin, 1993), *The Mystery of Shakespeare* by Charlton Ogburn (New York: Penguin, 1984), *A Dictionary of Shakespeare* by Stanley Wells (London: Oxford, 1998).

Printed in Canada

TABLE OF CONTENTS

Shakespeare...has been mutilated, mugged and masticated. He has been taken to the heights by some of our greatest actors, and to the depths by others. He has been translated, truncated, humiliated and musicalized. He has been quoted, quartered and pulverized; butchered, bullied and bashed beyond all recognition; misquoted and mismanaged; played by men, women and children whenever the fancy took them. He has challenged us all and won hands down. He has made fools of most of us at one time or another. There he stands, finger on cheek, quizzical, slightly bewildered, but passing the baton through century after century.

LAURENCE OLIVIER (1907-1989)

There is one book in the world of which it might be affirmed and argued, without fear of derision from any but the supreme and crowning fools among the foolishest of mankind, that it would be better for the world to lose all others and keep this one than to lose this and keep all other treasures bequeathed by human genius to all that we can conceive of eternity – to all that we can imagine of immortality. That book is best known, and best described for all of us, simply by the simple English name of its author. The word Shakespeare connotes more than any other man's name that ever was written or spoken upon earth.

ALGERNON CHARLES SWINBURNE (1837-1909)

MY BOOK OF MEMORY

– HENRY VI, PART ONE, II, iv, 101

read seen

☐ ☐ ALL'S WELL THAT ENDS WELL

☐ ☐ ANTONY AND CLEOPATRA

☐ ☐ AS YOU LIKE IT

☐ ☐ THE COMEDY OF ERRORS

☐ ☐ CORIOLANUS

☐ ☐ CYMBELINE

☐ ☐ HAMLET, PRINCE OF DENMARK

☐ ☐ JULIUS CAESAR

☐ ☐ KING HENRY IV, PART 1

☐ ☐ KING HENRY IV, PART 2

☐ ☐ KING HENRY V

☐ ☐ KING HENRY VI, PART 1

☐ ☐ KING HENRY VI, PART 2

☐ ☐ KING HENRY VI, PART 3

☐ ☐ KING HENRY VIII

☐ ☐ KING JOHN

☐ ☐ KING LEAR

☐ ☐ KING RICHARD II

☐ ☐ KING RICHARD III

☐ ☐ LOVE'S LABOUR'S LOST

☐ ☐ MACBETH

☐ ☐ MEASURE FOR MEASURE

☐ ☐ THE MERCHANT OF VENICE

read seen

☐ ☐   THE MERRY WIVES OF WINDSOR

☐ ☐   A MIDSUMMER NIGHT'S DREAM

☐ ☐   MUCH ADO ABOUT NOTHING

☐ ☐   OTHELLO, THE MOOR OF VENICE

☐ ☐   PERICLES, PRINCE OF TYRE

☐ ☐   ROMEO AND JULIET

☐ ☐   THE TAMING OF THE SHREW

☐ ☐   THE TEMPEST

☐ ☐   TIMON OF ATHENS

☐ ☐   TITUS ANDRONICUS

☐ ☐   TROILUS AND CRESSIDA

☐ ☐   TWELFTH NIGHT; OR, WHAT YOU WILL

☐ ☐   THE TWO GENTLEMEN OF VERONA

☐ ☐   THE TWO NOBLE KINSMEN

☐ ☐   THE WINTER'S TALE

THE POEMS

☐   A LOVER'S COMPLAINT

☐   THE PASSIONATE PILGRIM

☐   THE PHOENIX AND THE TURTLE

☐   THE RAPE OF LUCRECE

☐   SONNETS

☐   VENUS AND ADONIS

All's Well That Ends Well (1603)

THEATRE / TV / MOVIE	DATE

Antony and Cleopatra (1607)

THEATRE / TV / MOVIE	DATE

I remember, the Players have often mentioned it as an honour to Shakespeare that in his writing, (whatsoever he penned) he never blotted out a line. My answer hath been, would he had blotted a thousand. BEN JONSON (1572-1637)

As You Like It (1598)

THEATRE / TV / MOVIE	DATE

The Comedy of Errors (1592)

THEATRE / TV / MOVIE	DATE

Coriolanus (1608)

THEATRE / TV / MOVIE	DATE

Cymbeline (1609)

THEATRE / TV / MOVIE	DATE

*L*ook you, the good God himself naturally has a right to the first place, but the second certainly belongs to Shakespeare.   HEINRICH HEINE (1797-1856)

Hamlet, Prince of Denmark (1600-01)

THEATRE / TV / MOVIE	DATE

Julius Caesar (1599)

THEATRE / TV / MOVIE	DATE

King Henry IV, Part 1 (1597)

THEATRE / TV / MOVIE	DATE

King Henry IV, Part 2 (1598)

THEATRE / TV / MOVIE	DATE

King Henry V (1599)

THEATRE / TV / MOVIE	DATE

King Henry VIII (1613)

THEATRE / TV / MOVIE	DATE

King Henry VI, Part 1 (1590)

THEATRE / TV / MOVIE	DATE

King Henry VI, Part 2 (1590)

THEATRE / TV / MOVIE	DATE

King Henry VI, Part 3 (1591)

THEATRE / TV / MOVIE	DATE

King John (1596)

THEATRE / TV / MOVIE   DATE

_____

_____

_____

_____

_____

_____

_____

King Lear (1605)

THEATRE / TV / MOVIE   DATE

_____

_____

_____

_____

_____

_____

_____

I believe Shakespeare was not a whit more intelligible in his own day than he is now to an educated man, except for a few local allusions of no consequence. SAMUEL TAYLOR COLERIDGE (1772-1834)

King Richard II (1595)

THEATRE / TV / MOVIE	DATE

King Richard III (1592)

THEATRE / TV / MOVIE	DATE

 he man who of all modern, and perhaps ancient, poets had the largest and most comprehensive soul.

JOHN DRYDEN (1631-1700)

Love's Labour's Lost (1593)

THEATRE / TV / MOVIE	DATE

Macbeth (1606)

THEATRE / TV / MOVIE	DATE

Measure for Measure (1604)

THEATRE / TV / MOVIE   DATE

_____

_____

_____

_____

_____

_____

_____

_____

_____

_____

The Merchant of Venice (1596)

THEATRE / TV / MOVIE   DATE

_____

_____

_____

_____

_____

_____

_____

_____

_____

The Merry Wives of Windsor (1599)

THEATRE / TV / MOVIE   DATE

_____

_____

_____

_____

_____

_____

_____

_____

_____

A Midsummer Night's Dream (1594)

THEATRE / TV / MOVIE   DATE

_____

_____

_____

_____

_____

_____

_____

_____

_____

 hear a great deal, too, of Shakespeare, but I cannot read him, he is such a bombast fellow.

GEORGE III (1760-1820)

23

Much Ado About Nothing (1599)

THEATRE / TV / MOVIE	DATE

Othello, the Moor of Venice (1604)

THEATRE / TV / MOVIE	DATE

Pericles, Prince of Tyre (1608)

THEATRE / TV / MOVIE	DATE

Romeo and Juliet (1594-95)

THEATRE / TV / MOVIE	DATE

The Taming of the Shrew (1592)

THEATRE / TV / MOVIE	DATE

The Tempest (1611)

THEATRE / TV / MOVIE	DATE

Timon of Athens (11608)

THEATRE / TV / MOVIE	DATE

Titus Andronicus (1590-91)

THEATRE / TV / MOVIE	DATE

Troilus and Cressida (1602)

THEATRE / TV / MOVIE	DATE

Twelfth Night; or What You Will (1601)

THEATRE / TV / MOVIE	DATE

The Two Gentlemen of Verona (1592)

THEATRE / TV / MOVIE	DATE

The Two Noble Kinsmen (1613, written with John Fletcher)

THEATRE / TV / MOVIE   DATE

The Winter's Tale (1610)

THEATRE / TV / MOVIE   DATE

All men are impressed, in proportion to their own advancement in thought, by the genius of Shakespeare, and the greatest minds value him the most. RALPH WALDO EMERSON (1803-1882)

Shakespeare's name, you may depend on it, stands absurdly too high and will go down. He has no invention as to stories, none whatever. He took all his plots from old novels and threw their stories into a dramatic shape, at as little expense of thought as you or I could turn his plays back again into prose tales.... Suppose anyone to have had the dramatic handling for the first time of such ready-made stories as *Lear, Macbeth* & c. and he would be a sad fellow indeed if he did not make something very grand of them.

LORD BYRON (1788-1824)

THIS
GRACIOUS
SEASON

– CYMBELINE, V, v, 401

THIS GRACIOUS SEASON – A SHAKESPEAREAN FESTIVAL DIARY

YEAR

PLAYS OFFERED

_____

PLAY

DATE   TIME

THEATRE   SEATS

PLAY

DATE   TIME

THEATRE   SEATS

PLAY

DATE   TIME

THEATRE   SEATS

PLAY

DATE   TIME

THEATRE   SEATS

PLAY	
DATE	TIME
THEATRE	SEATS

PLAY	
DATE	TIME
THEATRE	SEATS

PLAY	
DATE	TIME
THEATRE	SEATS

PLAY	
DATE	TIME
THEATRE	SEATS

PLAY	
DATE	TIME
THEATRE	SEATS

he original writer is not the writer who thinks up a new story – there aren't any new stories, really – but the writer who tells one of the world's great stories in a new way. NORTHROP FRYE (1912-1991)

THIS GRACIOUS SEASON – A SHAKESPEAREAN FESTIVAL DIARY

YEAR

PLAYS OFFERED

PLAY

DATE   TIME

THEATRE   SEATS

PLAY

DATE   TIME

THEATRE   SEATS

PLAY

DATE   TIME

THEATRE   SEATS

PLAY

DATE   TIME

THEATRE   SEATS

PLAY

DATE

TIME

THEATRE

SEATS

PLAY

DATE

TIME

THEATRE

SEATS

PLAY

DATE

TIME

THEATRE

SEATS

PLAY

DATE

TIME

THEATRE

SEATS

PLAY

DATE

TIME

THEATRE

SEATS

PLAY

DATE

TIME

THEATRE

SEATS

YEAR

PLAYS OFFERED

PLAY

DATE   TIME

THEATRE   SEATS

PLAY

DATE   TIME

THEATRE   SEATS

hakespeare, coming upon me unawares, struck me like a thunderbolt. The lightning flash of that discovery revealed to me at a stroke the whole heaven of art, illuminating it to its remotest corners. I recognized the meaning of grandeur, beauty, dramatic truth, and I could measure the … pitiful narrowness of our own worn-out academic, cloistered traditions of poetry. HECTOR BERLIOZ (1803-1869)

PLAY

DATE   TIME

THEATRE   SEATS

PLAY

DATE   TIME

THEATRE   SEATS

PLAY

DATE   TIME

THEATRE   SEATS

PLAY

DATE   TIME

THEATRE   SEATS

PLAY

DATE   TIME

THEATRE   SEATS

PLAY

DATE   TIME

THEATRE   SEATS

YEAR

PLAYS OFFERED

PLAY

DATE   TIME

THEATRE   SEATS

PLAY

DATE   TIME

THEATRE   SEATS

PLAY

DATE   TIME

THEATRE   SEATS

PLAY

DATE   TIME

THEATRE   SEATS

PLAY	
DATE	TIME
THEATRE	SEATS

PLAY	
DATE	TIME
THEATRE	SEATS

PLAY	
DATE	TIME
THEATRE	SEATS

PLAY	
DATE	TIME
THEATRE	SEATS

When I read Shakespeare
    I am struck with wonder
That such trivial people
    should muse and thunder
In such lovely language.

D.H. LAWRENCE (1885-1930)

YEAR

PLAYS OFFERED

PLAY

DATE   TIME

THEATRE   SEATS

PLAY

DATE   TIME

THEATRE   SEATS

hakespeare, no mere child of nature: no automaton of genius, no passive vehicle of inspiration possessed by the spirit. Not possessing it; first studied patiently, meditated deeply, understood minutely, till knowledge, become habitual and intuitive, wedded itself to his habitual feelings, and at length gave birth to that stupendous power by which he stands alone, with no equal or second in his own class. SAMUEL TAYLOR COLERIDGE (1772-1834)

PLAY

DATE   TIME

THEATRE   SEATS

PLAY

DATE   TIME

THEATRE   SEATS

PLAY

DATE   TIME

THEATRE   SEATS

PLAY

DATE   TIME

THEATRE   SEATS

PLAY

DATE   TIME

THEATRE   SEATS

PLAY

DATE   TIME

THEATRE   SEATS

THIS GRACIOUS SEASON – A SHAKESPEAREAN FESTIVAL DIARY

YEAR

PLAYS OFFERED

PLAY

DATE   TIME

THEATRE   SEATS

PLAY

DATE   TIME

THEATRE   SEATS

PLAY

DATE   TIME

THEATRE   SEATS

PLAY

DATE   TIME

THEATRE   SEATS

PLAY

DATE   TIME

THEATRE   SEATS

PLAY

DATE   TIME

THEATRE   SEATS

PLAY

DATE   TIME

THEATRE   SEATS

PLAY

DATE   TIME

THEATRE   SEATS

PLAY

DATE   TIME

THEATRE   SEATS

PLAY

DATE   TIME

THEATRE   SEATS

THIS GRACIOUS SEASON – A SHAKESPEAREAN FESTIVAL DIARY

YEAR

PLAYS OFFERED

PLAY

DATE

TIME

THEATRE

SEATS

PLAY

DATE

TIME

THEATRE

SEATS

PLAY

DATE

TIME

THEATRE

SEATS

PLAY

DATE

TIME

THEATRE

SEATS

PLAY

DATE   TIME

THEATRE   SEATS

PLAY

DATE   TIME

THEATRE   SEATS

PLAY

DATE   TIME

THEATRE   SEATS

PLAY

DATE   TIME

THEATRE   SEATS

PLAY

DATE   TIME

THEATRE   SEATS

hakespeare is a drunken savage with some
imagination whose plays can please only
in London and Canada. VOLTAIRE (1694-1778)

YEAR

PLAYS OFFERED

PLAY

DATE   TIME

THEATRE   SEATS

he draft of his plays was in a manner intelligible, or they would not have been entertaining, to the penny-knaves who pestered the Globe and Blackfriars Theatre. But his profound reach of thought and his unrivalled knowledge of human nature were as far beyond the vulgar ken, as were the higher graces of his poetry. It is to men of sensibility and education that Shakespeare appeals as a man of genius; and it is to the literate class we must look for the impress of that genius.

C.M. INGLEBY, LLD, *SHAKESPEARE'S CENTURIE OF PRAYSE*,1874.

PLAY

DATE	TIME

THEATRE	SEATS

PLAY

DATE	TIME

THEATRE	SEATS

PLAY

DATE	TIME

THEATRE	SEATS

PLAY

DATE	TIME

THEATRE	SEATS

PLAY

DATE	TIME

THEATRE	SEATS

PLAY

DATE	TIME

THEATRE	SEATS

THIS GRACIOUS SEASON – A SHAKESPEAREAN FESTIVAL DIARY

YEAR

PLAYS OFFERED

PLAY

DATE .... TIME

THEATRE .... SEATS

PLAY

DATE .... TIME

THEATRE .... SEATS

PLAY

DATE .... TIME

THEATRE .... SEATS

PLAY

DATE .... TIME

THEATRE .... SEATS

PLAY

DATE   TIME

THEATRE   SEATS

PLAY

DATE   TIME

THEATRE   SEATS

PLAY

DATE   TIME

THEATRE   SEATS

PLAY

DATE   TIME

THEATRE   SEATS

PLAY

DATE   TIME

THEATRE   SEATS

PLAY

DATE   TIME

THEATRE   SEATS

THIS GRACIOUS SEASON – A SHAKESPEAREAN FESTIVAL DIARY

YEAR

PLAYS OFFERED

_____

_____

_____

_____

_____

_____

PLAY

DATE   TIME

THEATRE   SEATS

PLAY

DATE   TIME

THEATRE   SEATS

PLAY

DATE   TIME

THEATRE   SEATS

PLAY

DATE   TIME

THEATRE   SEATS

PLAY	
DATE	TIME
THEATRE	SEATS

PLAY	
DATE	TIME
THEATRE	SEATS

PLAY	
DATE	TIME
THEATRE	SEATS

I feel that our fetish [with Shakespeare] is safe for three centuries yet. The bust too – there in the Stratford Church. The precious bust, the calm bust, the serene bust, the emotionless bust, with the dandy mustache and the putty face, unseamed of care – the face which looked passionlessly down upon the awed pilgrims for a hundred and fifty years and will still look down upon the awed pilgrims three hundred more, with the deep, deep, deep, subtle, subtle, subtle, expression of a bladder.   MARK TWAIN (1835-1910)

With the single exception of Homer, there is no eminent writer, not even Sir Walter Scott, whom I can despise so entirely as I despise Shakespeare when I measure my mind against his. The intensity of my impatience with him occasionally reaches such a pitch, that it would positively be a relief to me to dig him up and throw stones at him, knowing as I do how incapable he and his worshippers are of understanding any less obvious form of indignity.

GEORGE BERNARD SHAW (1856-1950),
AFTER SEEING IRVING'S PRODUCTION OF *CYMBELINE*

MADAM, HOW LIKE YOU THIS PLAY?

– HAMLET, III, ii, 239

PLAY

THEATRE

DATE

CAST

REVIEW

PLAY

THEATRE

DATE

CAST

REVIEW

PLAY

THEATRE

DATE

CAST

REVIEW

PLAY

THEATRE

DATE

CAST

REVIEW

PLAY

THEATRE

DATE

CAST

REVIEW

PLAY

THEATRE

DATE

CAST

REVIEW

T is ten to one this play can never please All that are here: some come to take their ease, And sleep an act or two: but those, we fear, We have frightened with our trumpets; so 'tis clear, They'll say 'tis naught: others to hear the city Abus'd extremely, and to cry, – That's witty! Which we have not done neither.

KING HENRY VIII, EPILOGUE

PLAY

THEATRE

DATE

CAST

REVIEW

PLAY

THEATRE

DATE

CAST

REVIEW

PLAY

THEATRE

DATE

CAST

REVIEW

PLAY

THEATRE

DATE

CAST

REVIEW

PLAY

THEATRE

DATE

CAST

REVIEW

PLAY

THEATRE

DATE

CAST

REVIEW

PLAY

THEATRE

DATE

CAST

REVIEW

PLAY

THEATRE

DATE

CAST

REVIEW

PLAY

THEATRE

DATE

CAST

REVIEW

PLAY

THEATRE

DATE

CAST

REVIEW

acbeth is a tale told by a genius, full of soundness and fury, signifying many things.

JAMES THURBER

PLAY

THEATRE

DATE

CAST

REVIEW

PLAY

THEATRE

DATE

CAST

REVIEW

PLAY

THEATRE

DATE

CAST

REVIEW

PLAY

THEATRE

DATE

CAST

REVIEW

PLAY

THEATRE

DATE

CAST

REVIEW

*C*incinnati, April 2nd, 1849: Acted Hamlet to a rather rickety audience, but I tried my utmost, and engaged the attention of at least the greater part of the auditory. In the scene after the play with Rosencrantz and Guildenstern an occurrence took place that, for disgusting brutality, indecent outrage, and malevolent barbarism, must be without parallel in the theatre of any civilized community. Whilst speaking to them about 'the pipe,' a ruffian from the left side of the gallery threw into the middle of the stage the half of the raw carcase of a sheep! *THE DIARIES OF WILLIAM CHARLES MACREADY* 1833-1851, ED. WILLIAM TOYNBEE, 1912

PLAY

THEATRE

DATE

CAST

REVIEW

PLAY

THEATRE

DATE

CAST

REVIEW

PLAY

THEATRE

DATE

CAST

REVIEW

PLAY

THEATRE

DATE

CAST

REVIEW

PLAY

THEATRE

DATE

CAST

REVIEW

PLAY

THEATRE

DATE

CAST

REVIEW

PLAY

THEATRE

DATE

CAST

REVIEW

PLAY

THEATRE

DATE

CAST

REVIEW

PLAY

THEATRE

DATE

CAST

REVIEW

PLAY

THEATRE

DATE

CAST

REVIEW

The only plays that really interest me are the ones that drive me nuts. I don't believe that Shakespeare is any more contradictory, confusing, or ambiguous than people are in life. He's only dramatizing what actually goes on. That's why he is the ultimate realistic writer. TONY CHURCH

PLAY

THEATRE

DATE

CAST

REVIEW

PLAY

THEATRE

DATE

CAST

REVIEW

PLAY

THEATRE

DATE

CAST

REVIEW

PLAY

THEATRE

DATE

CAST

REVIEW

PLAY

THEATRE

DATE

CAST

REVIEW

When people come to see a Shakespeare play they almost invariably come with an expectation – they've read it, they've heard about it, or they've probably seen other productions – and that anticipation is one of the most useful things for a director. Because once you know what an audience anticipates, you can frustrate those expectations and re-angle them in interesting ways. What's interesting is not the beaten path, but how one creates highways and detours using the plays as starting points.

CHARLES MAROWITZ

PLAY

THEATRE

DATE

CAST

REVIEW

PLAY

THEATRE

DATE

CAST

REVIEW

hildren, set to act Shakespeare, will fling themselves innocently at the greatest of the plays; and, just because they do not comprehend and so cannot subdue the characters to their own likeness, they let us see them – though diminished and feeble – as through a clear glass. For the matured actor it is not quite so easy. He must comprehend the character, identify himself with it, and then – forget himself in it.

HARLEY GRANVILLE BARKER (1877-1946)

THESE ARE
THE PLAYERS

– HAMLET, II, ii, 386

ACTOR / ROLE

PLAY

THEATRE / TV / MOVIE

PRODUCTION NOTES

REVIEW

ACTOR / ROLE

PLAY

THEATRE / TV / MOVIE

PRODUCTION NOTES

REVIEW

ACTOR / ROLE

PLAY

THEATRE / TV / MOVIE

PRODUCTION NOTES

REVIEW

ACTOR / ROLE

PLAY

THEATRE / TV / MOVIE

PRODUCTION NOTES

REVIEW

ACTOR / ROLE

PLAY

THEATRE / TV / MOVIE

PRODUCTION NOTES

REVIEW

ACTOR / ROLE

PLAY

THEATRE / TV / MOVIE

PRODUCTION NOTES

REVIEW

ACTOR / ROLE

PLAY

THEATRE / TV / MOVIE

PRODUCTION NOTES

REVIEW

ACTOR / ROLE

PLAY

THEATRE / TV / MOVIE

PRODUCTION NOTES

REVIEW

Whenever an actor comes to [Shakespeare], he should come with a hunger and excitement. To make his language work from your brain to your fingertips is to fulfil your profession. You can come back to him time and time again, attacking the same role, and there will always be something new to discover. They say that even a bad actor playing Hamlet will get something right. LAURENCE OLIVIER

ACTOR / ROLE

PLAY

THEATRE / TV / MOVIE

PRODUCTION NOTES

REVIEW

ACTOR / ROLE

PLAY

THEATRE / TV / MOVIE

PRODUCTION NOTES

REVIEW

ACTOR / ROLE

PLAY

THEATRE / TV / MOVIE

PRODUCTION NOTES

REVIEW

ACTOR / ROLE

PLAY

THEATRE / TV / MOVIE

PRODUCTION NOTES

REVIEW

ACTOR / ROLE

PLAY

THEATRE / TV / MOVIE

PRODUCTION NOTES

REVIEW

ACTOR / ROLE

PLAY

THEATRE / TV / MOVIE

PRODUCTION NOTES

REVIEW

ACTOR / ROLE

PLAY

THEATRE / TV / MOVIE

PRODUCTION NOTES

REVIEW

ACTOR / ROLE

PLAY

THEATRE / TV / MOVIE

PRODUCTION NOTES

REVIEW

ccording to the legend, one of the grenadiers [on guard at the stage-doors during the Garrick period] was so overcome by the acting of Garrick as Lear that he fainted in full view of the audience; Garrick, deeply touched by this tribute to his powers, rewarded the fellow with a guinea. Naturally, word of this generosity spread, and the next night of Garrick's acting another guard dropped down at his post. Only that night Garrick was acting a comedy! GEORGE C.D. ODELL, *SHAKESPEARE FROM BETTERTON TO IRVING*, 1921

THESE ARE THE PLAYERS – BY ACTOR

ACTOR / ROLE

PLAY

THEATRE / TV / MOVIE

PRODUCTION NOTES

REVIEW

ACTOR / ROLE

PLAY

THEATRE / TV / MOVIE

PRODUCTION NOTES

REVIEW

ACTOR / ROLE

PLAY

THEATRE / TV / MOVIE

PRODUCTION NOTES

REVIEW

ACTOR / ROLE

PLAY

THEATRE / TV / MOVIE

PRODUCTION NOTES

REVIEW

ACTOR / ROLE

PLAY

THEATRE / TV / MOVIE

PRODUCTION NOTES

REVIEW

ACTOR / ROLE

PLAY

THEATRE / TV / MOVIE

PRODUCTION NOTES

REVIEW

ACTOR / ROLE

PLAY

THEATRE / TV / MOVIE

PRODUCTION NOTES

REVIEW

ACTOR / ROLE

PLAY

THEATRE / TV / MOVIE

PRODUCTION NOTES

REVIEW

*E*dmund Kean cared less for delineating human nature than he did for making a point tell; and never asked what sort of a character he was to represent, but what sort of a part he was to play – not what individual he should delineate, but what effects he should produce. King Lear was to him only an admirable medium of obtaining applause, and valued in proportion to that applause. LEMAN REDE, QUOTED IN B.W. PROCTER (BARRY CORNWALL), *THE LIFE OF EDMUND KEAN*, 1835

ACTOR / ROLE

PLAY

THEATRE / TV / MOVIE

PRODUCTION NOTES

REVIEW

ACTOR / ROLE

PLAY

THEATRE / TV / MOVIE

PRODUCTION NOTES

REVIEW

ACTOR / ROLE

PLAY

THEATRE / TV / MOVIE

PRODUCTION NOTES

REVIEW

THESE ARE THE PLAYERS – BY ROLE

ROLE

ACTOR

PRODUCTION

RATING

ROLE

ACTOR

PRODUCTION

RATING

ROLE

ACTOR

PRODUCTION

RATING

ROLE

ACTOR

PRODUCTION

RATING

ROLE

ACTOR

PRODUCTION

RATING

ROLE

ACTOR

PRODUCTION

RATING

ROLE

ACTOR

PRODUCTION

RATING

ROLE

ACTOR

PRODUCTION

RATING

f the playwright is blessed with infinite generosity, if he is not obsessed with his own ideas, he will give the impression that he is in total sympathy with everyone. Beyond that, if there are twenty characters and the playwright manages to invest each one with the same power of conviction, we come to the miracle of Shakespeare. A computer would have difficulty in programming all the points of view his plays contain. PETER BROOK

ROLE

ACTOR

PRODUCTION

RATING

ROLE

ACTOR

PRODUCTION

RATING

ROLE

ACTOR

PRODUCTION

RATING

ROLE

ACTOR

PRODUCTION

RATING

ROLE

ACTOR

PRODUCTION

RATING

ROLE

ACTOR

PRODUCTION

RATING

ROLE

ACTOR

PRODUCTION

RATING

ROLE

ACTOR

PRODUCTION

RATING

ROLE

ACTOR

PRODUCTION

RATING

ROLE

ACTOR

PRODUCTION

RATING

THESE ARE THE PLAYERS – BY ROLE

ROLE

ACTOR

PRODUCTION

RATING

ROLE

ACTOR

PRODUCTION

RATING

ROLE

ACTOR

PRODUCTION

RATING

ROLE

ACTOR

PRODUCTION

RATING

The stage can be defined as a place where Shakespeare murdered Hamlet and a great many Hamlets have since murdered Shakespeare.

ROBERT MORSE

ROLE

ACTOR

PRODUCTION

RATING

ROLE

ACTOR

PRODUCTION

RATING

ROLE

ACTOR

PRODUCTION

RATING

ROLE

ACTOR

PRODUCTION

RATING

ROLE

ACTOR

PRODUCTION

RATING

THESE ARE THE PLAYERS – BY ROLE

ROLE

ACTOR

PRODUCTION

RATING

ROLE

ACTOR

PRODUCTION

RATING

ROLE

ACTOR

PRODUCTION

RATING

ROLE

ACTOR

PRODUCTION

RATING

ROLE

ACTOR

PRODUCTION

RATING

ROLE

ACTOR

PRODUCTION

RATING

ROLE

ACTOR

PRODUCTION

RATING

ROLE

ACTOR

PRODUCTION

RATING

ROLE

ACTOR

PRODUCTION

RATING

he trouble with Shakespeare is that you
never get to sit down unless you are a king.

GEORGE S. KAUFMAN

THESE ARE THE PLAYERS – BY ROLE

ROLE

ACTOR

PRODUCTION

RATING

ROLE

ACTOR

PRODUCTION

RATING

ROLE

ACTOR

PRODUCTION

RATING

ROLE

ACTOR

PRODUCTION

RATING

ROLE

ACTOR

PRODUCTION

RATING

ROLE

ACTOR

PRODUCTION

RATING

ROLE

ACTOR

PRODUCTION

RATING

ROLE

ACTOR

PRODUCTION

RATING

ROLE

ACTOR

PRODUCTION

RATING

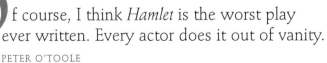 f course, I think *Hamlet* is the worst play
ever written. Every actor does it out of vanity.

PETER O'TOOLE

Isn't it odd, when you think of it, that you may list all the celebrated Englishman, Irishmen, and Scotchmen of modern times, clear back to the first Tudors – a list containing five hundred names, shall we say? – and you can go to the histories, biographies, and cyclopedia and learn the particulars of the lives of every one of them. Every one of them except one – the most famous, the most renowned – by far the most illustrious of them all – Shakespeare!... About him you can find nothing. Nothing of even the slightest importance. Nothing worth the trouble of storing away in your memory. Nothing that even remotely indicates that he was ever anything more than a distinctly commonplace person.

MARK TWAIN

THOU STAR
OF POETS

– BEN JONSON, FIRST FOLIO

_I_ n the…debates I argued for the theory that King James himself was the real poet who used the _nom de plume_ Shakespeare. King James was brilliant. He was the greatest king who ever sat on the British throne. Who else among royalty, in his time, would have the giant talent to write Shakespeare's works?

MALCOLM LITTLE (LATER MALCOLM X)

am "sort of haunted" by the conviction that the divine William is the biggest and most successful fraud ever practised on a patient world. The more I turn him round and round the more he so affects me... I find it *almost* as impossible to conceive that Bacon wrote the plays as to conceive that the man from Stratford, as we know the man from Stratford, did.

HENRY JAMES (1843-1916)

FAVORITE HISTORY PLAYS

King Henry IV, Part 1

King Henry IV, Part 2

King Henry V

King Henry VI, Part 1

King Henry VI, Part 2

King Henry VI, Part 3

King Henry VIII

King John

King Richard II

King Richard III

FAVORITE TRAGEDIES

Antony and Cleopatra

Coriolanus

Hamlet

Julius Caesar

King Lear

Macbeth

Othello

Romeo and Juliet

Timon of Athens

Titus Andronicus

Troilus and Cressida

FAVORITE COMEDIES

All's Well That Ends Well

As You Like It

The Comedy of Errors

Love's Labour's Lost

Measure for Measure

The Merchant of Venice

The Merry Wives of Windsor

A Midsummer Night's Dream

Much Ado About Nothing

The Taming of the Shrew

Twelfth Night

The Two Gentlemen of Verona

FAVORITE ROMANCES

Cymbeline

Pericles, Prince of Tyre

The Tempest

The Two Noble Kinsmen

The Winter's Tale

I don't know if Bacon wrote the works of Shakespeare, but if he did not, he missed the opportunity of his life. SIR JAMES BARRIE (1869-1937)

MY DREAM CAST FOR

CAST

MY DREAM CAST FOR

CAST

MY DREAM CAST FOR

CAST

MY DREAM CAST FOR

CAST

MY DREAM CAST FOR

CAST

MY DREAM CAST FOR

CAST

MY DREAM CAST FOR

CAST

MY DREAM CAST FOR

CAST

MY DREAM CAST FOR

CAST

If Bacon wrote Shakespeare, who wrote Bacon?

WILLIAM KITTREDGE

107

The Elizabethan theatre was a similar set-up to Hollywood in many respects. Collective writing, rapid writing on commission, repeated re-use of the same subjects, no control for writers over their own products, fame only among other writers, then the passion-filled action, the plots, the new settings, the political interests, etc. Support by the aristocracy is over and the box office becomes decisive; class differences become more acute, the public is made up of irreconcilable classes, the highest and the lowest (the middle group is tied up between 2 and 5 in the afternoon). Even Shakespeare's curious retirement to run a public house resembles the escape to the ranch that everybody here is planning.

BERTOLT BRECHT (1898-1956)

MANY AGES
HENCE

_I_ read Shakespeare directly [after] I have finished writing. When my mind is agape and red and hot. Then it is astonishing. I never yet knew how amazing his stretch and speed and word coining power is, until I felt it utterly outpace and outrace my own.... Even the lesser known plays are written at a speed that is quicker than anybody else's quickest....Why then should any-one else attempt to write? VIRGINIA WOOLF (1882-1941)

TITLE

AUTHOR

PUBLISHER

TITLE

AUTHOR

PUBLISHER

TITLE

AUTHOR

PUBLISHER

TITLE

AUTHOR

PUBLISHER

TITLE

AUTHOR

PUBLISHER

TITLE

AUTHOR

PUBLISHER

TITLE

AUTHOR

PUBLISHER

TITLE

AUTHOR

PUBLISHER

TITLE

AUTHOR

PUBLISHER

TITLE

AUTHOR

PUBLISHER

TITLE

AUTHOR

PUBLISHER

TITLE

AUTHOR

PUBLISHER

TITLE

AUTHOR

PUBLISHER

TITLE

AUTHOR

PUBLISHER

TITLE

AUTHOR

PUBLISHER

TITLE

AUTHOR

PUBLISHER

TITLE

AUTHOR

PUBLISHER

To know the force of human genius we should read Shakespeare; to see the insignificance of human learning we may study his commentators.

WILLIAM HAZLITT (1778-1830)

TITLE

AUTHOR

PUBLISHER

TITLE

AUTHOR

PUBLISHER

TITLE

AUTHOR

PUBLISHER

TITLE

AUTHOR

PUBLISHER

TITLE

AUTHOR

PUBLISHER

TITLE

AUTHOR

PUBLISHER

Shakespeare one gets acquainted with without knowing how. It is a part of an Englishman's constitution. His thoughts and beauties are so spread abroad that one touches them everywhere; one is intimate with him by instinct. No man of any brain can open at a good part of one of his plays without falling into the flow of his meaning immediately.

JANE AUSTEN, *MANSFIELD PARK*

nce I sat upon a promontory, And heard a mermaid, on a dolphin's back, Uttering such dulcet and harmonious breath, That the rude sea grew civil at her song, And certain stars shot madly from their spheres, To hear the sea maid's music.

A MIDSUMMER NIGHT'S DREAM, II, i, 149

_I_ f Shakespeare were alive now, no doubt he'd be interviewed every week and his opinions canvassed on every subject from national foreign policy to the social effects of punk rock. But in his day nobody cared what Shakespeare's views were about anything, and he wouldn't have been allowed to discuss public affairs publicly. NORTHROP FRYE

If you cannot understand my argument, and declare 'It's all Greek to me', you're quoting Shakespeare; if you claim to be more sinned against than sinning, you are quoting Shakespeare; if you recall your salad days, you are quoting Shakespeare; if you act more in sorrow than in anger, ... even if you bid me good riddance and send me packing, if you wish I was dead as a doornail, if you think I am an eyesore, a laughing stock, the devil incarnate, a stony-hearted villain, bloody-minded or a blinking idiot, then – by Jove! O Lord! Tut, tut! For goodness' sake! What the dickens! But me no buts – it is all one to me, for you are quoting Shakespeare.

BERNARD LEVIN, *ENTHUSIASMS* (1983)

BETHUMPED
WITH WORDS

– *KING JOHN*, II, i, 466

Shakespeare was so facile in employing words that he was able to use over 7,200 of them – more than occur in the whole King James version of the Bible – only once and never again. LOUIS MARDER

man can be forgiven a lot if he can quote
Shakespeare in an economic crisis. PRINCE PHILIP

Will a dab of Shakespeare daintily perfume my wit or just sound like the literary belching of a compulsive nerd? GARY TAYLOR

I believe that this [theatre] is a place of illumination, a place where the values of our civilization are constantly displayed and discussed.... I believe that if there is no place to discuss on Shakespeare's level the problems of mankind, something is going to happen to us as a species.... This theatre can be instrumental – as it has been for many years – in helping the survival. It can help to hold back the darkness, to keep a candle aglow, in this horrendous universe we are living in.

JOHN HIRSCH (1930-1989)

THIS
WOODEN O

– HENRY V, Prologue, 11

THEATRE

LOCATION   PHONE

NOTES

_____

_____

_____

_____

_____

_____

_____

THEATRE

LOCATION   PHONE

NOTES

_____

_____

_____

_____

_____

_____

_____

THEATRE

LOCATION   PHONE

NOTES

_____

_____

_____

_____

_____

_____

THEATRE

LOCATION   PHONE

NOTES

THEATRE

LOCATION   PHONE

NOTES

---

ost [people] have this notion that classical culture has to be good for you.... I have directed some of these plays several times, and I still don't understand them. But you're not meant to *understand* Shakespeare! Everyone thinks that at the end of an art experience they have to answer twenty questions and get nineteen right. No! What matters is your own personal interaction with the play.... It's like life. There's enough there for everyone to find something for themselves. PETER SELLARS

THEATRE

LOCATION   PHONE

NOTES

_____

_____

_____

_____

_____

_____

_____

THEATRE

LOCATION   PHONE

NOTES

_____

_____

_____

_____

_____

_____

_____

THEATRE

LOCATION   PHONE

NOTES

_____

_____

_____

_____

_____

THEATRE

LOCATION   PHONE

NOTES

THEATRE

LOCATION   PHONE

NOTES

THEATRE

LOCATION   PHONE

NOTES

THEATRE

LOCATION   PHONE

NOTES

_____

_____

_____

_____

_____

_____

THEATRE

LOCATION   PHONE

NOTES

_____

_____

_____

_____

_____

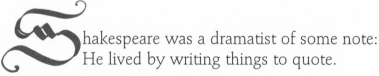

hakespeare was a dramatist of some note:
He lived by writing things to quote.

H.C. BRUNNER